Presented To:

_____

From:

_____

Date:

_____

I Am That!

Prayers and Affirmations for Successful Living

Dr. Lucille Farrell-Scott
& Dr. Sunne-Ryse S. Smith

Copyright © 2020 by Dr. Lucille P. Farrell-Scott and Dr. Sunne-Ryse S. Smith.

All rights reserved. No part of this book may be reproduced in any written, electronic, recording, or photocopying without written permission of the publisher or author. The exception would be in the case of brief quotations embodied on the pages where the publisher or author specifically grants permission.

Books may be purchased in quantity and/or special sales by contacting the author.

Published by
Mynd Matters Publishing
715 Peachtree Street NE, Suites 100 & 200
Atlanta, GA 30308
www.myndmatterspublishing.com

978-1-953307-22-4 (Pbk)

SECOND EDITION

CONTENTS

FOREWORD 7
INTRODUCTION 9
A MORNING PRAYER 11
PRAYER FOR HEALTH 18
PRAYER FOR INCREASE 25
PRAYER FOR PROTECTION 32
PRAYER FOR GOD'S PRESENCE 39
PRAYER FOR COURAGE 46
PRAYER FOR PEACE 53
PRAYER OF THANKSGIVING 60
PRAYER FOR LOVE OF SELF 67
PRAYER FOR ENTREPRENEURS 74
PRAYER FOR FAITH 81
PRAYER FOR LOVE FROM OTHERS 88
PRAYER FOR COMFORT 95
PRAYER FOR GUIDANCE 102
PRAYER FOR CONFIDENCE 109
PRAYER FOR SPOUSES 116
PRAYER FOR PARENTS 123
PRAYER FOR SEEKING A SPOUSE 130
CREATING YOUR OWN "I AM" STATEMENTS 137
WRITE YOUR OWN "I AM" STATEMENTS 139
ABOUT THE AUTHORS 141

FOREWORD

You are holding this book right now because at this very moment in your life, you have an opportunity to transform your world with the power of your spoken word.

If you are ready to have a life of purpose, passion, peace and prosperity and live a life of joy and abundance, the pages of this book contain the "tools for building the consciousness" required to attract all that you desire and require into your life. The tools for building consciousness for which I refer to are "affirmations." An affirmation is a powerful word of truth that when spoken about you with compassion, conviction and deep feeling, makes firm in your own awareness the truth that you have spoken. As a result, you change how you see yourself, how you feel about yourself, and how you act.

When you have had a shift in consciousness, the energy and the atmosphere that radiates from within and around you draws into your experience, manifestations that reflect the new consciousness or mindset that you have established through your affirmations!

This is not hocus pocus or magical thinking. This is a lawful process and is always at work, whether we are conscious of it or not. We are always having what we say. Actually, you are always "saying or declaring" your world into being, whether it be audible or inaudible. The deep intention and feeling behind what you say inwardly, within the privacy of your own soul is being transmitted into your experience. This is why my dear friends Dr. Lucille Farrell-Scott and Dr.

Sunne-Ryse Smith have brought you this important book. They are passionate about showing people how to unleash the power of the spoken word to call into their lives abundance in all of its forms.

By uncovering and using the mystical power of the "I AM" principle, you are aligning your life with the authority that governs the entire universe and unleashing it in a positive way for you. Your use of "I AM" is always symbolic of the following formula:

$$I + A = M$$

Essentially, your Intention (I) plus your Attention (A) equals your Manifestation (M). This is why it is very important for you to be conscious of your every word because you are giving an account for it every time your intention is manifested. Think of it this way, if your words were diamonds, wouldn't you be more intentional and attentive to how you used them?

Let my friends lead you through a simple, yet profound process for transforming your life. Every page will be a self-guided journey to inspire and empower you to design and live the life of your dreams!

-Kevin Kitrell Ross
Bestselling author of *The Courageous Conversations* series and *The Optimistic Seed*

INTRODUCTION

This book is a simple guide to help you build your confidence. By using "I AM" affirmations, you begin to see yourself beyond your challenges, hurts, and present circumstances.

How many times a day do you use the statement "I am…?" What words do you put after "I am?" Whatever you say after your "I am" becomes your internal dialogue that eventually manifests in your daily experiences.

Do this quick exercise. Look in the mirror and complete the following statement aloud using five different adjectives:

I AM  .

What did you say? When you looked in the mirror, what did you see? How did you describe yourself? What initial attributes came to mind? It is likely the first few adjectives you used were about your external appearance—race, gender, height, and weight? But after all that can be seen, who are you? It is important to understand that you are more than your gender. You are much more than the numbers on a weight scale. You are an outward expression of your deepest thoughts, emotions, and inward beliefs that you hold to be true about yourself.

In the Old Testament of the Bible, Moses was instructed to lead the children of Israel out of bondage. He asked God, "Behold, when I come unto the children of Israel, and shall say unto them, The God of your fathers hath sent me unto you; and they shall say to me, what is his name? What shall I say unto them?"

God replied, "I AM THAT I AM: and he said, Thus shalt thou say unto the children of Israel, *I AM* hath sent me unto you." In that one passage, God used one name—I AM. In that name was everything the children of Israel ever needed.

> **WHAT YOU *SEE* ABOUT YOURSELF IS WHAT YOU *SAY* ABOUT YOURSELF.**

In the New Testament, Jesus followed God's example by using "I am" statements to describe who he was to God's people: "I am the bread of life," "I am the good shepherd," "I am the light of the world."

These are just three of the seven "I Am" statements Jesus used to reveal the relationship between God and man. The question for you is what do you put after your "I Am"? What are you calling yourself?

This book will transform your self-image and revolutionize your life. The included affirmations are to be used based on your personal needs and desires. Once you select your affirmations and prayers, commit to saying them while looking in the mirror, twice a day for thirty days. Make a decision to see yourself the way God sees you.

A Morning Prayer

No matter how difficult life may appear, take joy in knowing you are alive. You are still breathing. This fact indicates that God has a plan for your life. Forget the mistakes of yesterday and embrace the reality of now, the reality that you are here to experience another day. Every sunrise you see is a gift of endless possibilities. Appreciate that gift.

*Let everything that hath breath,
praise ye the Lord.*

-Psalm 150:6

I AM AWAKE

I Am awake! I Am alive!

I Am living! I Am life! I Am full of life!

This is the day God has made just for me and I Am rejoicing in this day!

God started this day with me on His mind and I woke up excited to welcome this new day.

I Am alive and awake to walk out the promise of this beautiful day!

Today I Am a tree planted by streams of water.

Like the tree brings forth fruit, I experience success in all my endeavors.

Everything that will occur today helps me blossom.

I Am a flower coming into bud!

I have been given another opportunity to live my best life and I will.

I stretch my hands wide and I proclaim for everyone to hear…

I Am full of life!

I Am life!

I Am living!

I Am awake!

I Am alive!

I Am that! That is who I Am!

Thoughts, Revelation, Prayers

Thoughts, Revelation, Prayers

Thoughts, Revelation, Prayers

Thoughts, Revelation, Prayers

Prayer for Health

Your body is a perfectly crafted masterpiece created by God. Every system has its own unique and independent function, yet cannot function independently. Your genetic code is God's stamp of approval on your existence. You must honor your body. It is the vehicle, given by God, to transport you through your life journey.

I will praise thee, for I am fearfully and wonderfully made…

-Psalm 139:14

I AM HEALTH

I Am health! I Am physically strong!

I Am full of vigor! I Am whole!

I Am made in the image of my Father and He is health, therefore I Am health.

I was created to embrace health in all of its glory.

God's will is for me to live in perfect health. I accept His will for my life.

So, where there is dis-ease, I thank God for giving me restored health.

I take health in my arms and I embrace it by eating the right foods and enjoying daily exercise.

I love health! I make daily decisions to honor my health!

I release any hidden emotions that will foster illness to live and grow in my body.

I take care of my body so my body can take care of me.

I proclaim loudly to the universe that I Am health, knowing the universe will render to me that which I say!

I Am whole!

I Am physically strong!

I Am health!

I Am that! That is who I Am!

Thoughts, Revelation, Prayers

Thoughts, Revelation, Prayers

Thoughts, Revelation, Prayers

Thoughts, Revelation, Prayers

Prayer for Increase

There has never been a time when oxygen was not available to mankind. Air is available to all of us. God's plan is for people to always have what they need to survive.

Accept that the universe is abundant. Think about wealth the way you would think about air. It is all around you and you have access to it just like oxygen. You do not wake up worrying that one day there will be no more oxygen. You just breathe. Breathe in wealth and provision in the same manner.

Therefore I say unto you, take no thought for your life, what ye shall eat; neither for the body, what ye shall put on.

-Luke 12:22

I AM WEALTH

I Am wealth! I Am affluent!

I Am rich!

God's plan for me includes being an heir to His kingdom!

God does not discriminate.

He gives the earth the ability to produce in abundance.

All nature sings of the wealth of God.

As His offspring, I have the same ability and I too, sing of the wealth of God.

I Am wealth, unadulterated wealth!

I lack nothing! I shall not want!

The resources of the universe are at my disposal and I take advantage of those resources every day.

Today God blesses me and multiplies my supplies.

Wealth is fluid and I Am always in its flow.

As wealth flows to me, I experience it and freely share with others.

I speak to wealth with love and peace because I know however I treat wealth, wealth will treat me.

I live, move, and have my total existence in the wealth of my Father.

I Am rich!

I Am affluent!

I Am wealth!

I Am that! That is who I Am!

Thoughts, Revelation, Prayers

Thoughts, Revelation, Prayers

Thoughts, Revelation, Prayers

Thoughts, Revelation, Prayers

Prayer for Protection

You probably have a lock on the doors of your house and your car. To get into your email, an ATM, and your laptop, you have passwords and security questions set-up to protect your information.

Do you know that you are just as valuable to God as your bank account is to you? Psalm 23 is one of the most commonly used scriptures of protection. "Yea thou I walk through the valley of the shadow of death, I will fear no evil...thy rod (represents protection) and thy staff (represents guidance), they comfort me." No matter where you go today, you are protected.

For in the time of trouble he shall hide me in his pavilion: in the secret of his tabernacle shall he hide me; he shall set me up upon a rock.

-Psalm 27:5

I AM PROTECTED

I Am protected! I Am safe!

I Am covered!

Under God's wings, I Am sheltered.

Just as a hen covers her chicks and protects them from harm, I put my whole trust in God's ability to protect me, my home, my children, and anything that concerns me.

I proclaim, God is my refuge, my safety net, my fortress, my high tower.

I Am protected.

The storms and winds of life may blow today, but I am shielded.

Angels have been commanded to guard and defend me.

They are constantly surrounding me.

I have a banner and a covering that keeps me protected.

I know God is ordering my steps.

I do not doubt that I will reach my destination.

God has engraved me in the palm of His hands.

I Am the apple of His eye and He always watches over me.

I Am covered!

I Am safe!

I AM protected!

I Am that! That is who I Am!

Thoughts, Revelation, Prayers

Thoughts, Revelation, Prayers

Thoughts, Revelation, Prayers

Thoughts, Revelation, Prayers

# Prayer for God's Presence

Being aware that there is a higher power at work in your life is a liberating feeling. When you quiet yourself and think about the fact that God is in love with you and concerned about your life, you enter into His presence.

Turn off the noise of the world and experience God. Let go of every care, concern, or worry and allow the presence of God to guide you into joy and peace. In this place of stillness and silence, you find your voice.

Thou wilt show me the path of life: in thy presence is fullness of joy; at thy right hand there are pleasures for evermore.

-Psalm 16:11

I AM SILENT

I Am silent! I Am quiet!

I Am still!

Today I take this moment to be silent.

For I know that he who has the ability not to speak in time of turmoil, has the wherewithal to conquer any adverse situation.

So I embrace this quietness and serenity of God.

I enter into His presence knowing in this place, He will guide me in decisions about my home, my family, and my life.

Here in this silence, in His presence, there is fullness of joy.

For that, I Am content.

I Am calm in His presence knowing all is well.

For that, I Am content.

As I meditate on the silence of the mountains, their stillness brings quiet to my soul.

I ask you God to speak in this stillness.

I wait.

I Am still!

I Am quiet!

I AM silent!

I Am that! That is who I Am!

Thoughts, Revelation, Prayers

Thoughts, Revelation, Prayers

Thoughts, Revelation, Prayers

Thoughts, Revelation, Prayers

Prayer for Courage

When you think of courage, you may think of the "Cowardly Lion" from the Wizard of Oz. He wanted the Wizard of Oz to give him courage. He did not realize that the courage he desired was always within him.

Maybe you feel as though you are faced with a difficult decision or situation. Recognize that everything you need to overcome is resting in you. God made you fearless. Your courage is manifested in your "going through" the trials and tribulations. You won't know your true power until you rise up and be bold in the moment of fear.

*Wait on the Lord: be of good courage,
and he shall strengthen thine heart:
wait, I say, on the Lord.*

-Psalm 27:14

I AM COURAGEOUS

I Am courageous! I Am bold!
I Am fearless! I Am brave!
I Am very courageous and valiant!
So today, I move to the next level.
I make the decision to remove all limits from my thinking, speaking, and being.
I Am courageous!
I do not shrink in the face of adversity.
I walk without fear because God did not create me with a spirit of fear.
He gave me the ability to mount up with wings like eagles.
So I soar into my destiny without fear or doubt.
I know God has great plans for my life and I will accomplish those plans today.
God takes pleasure in my success.
Today I Am more than a conqueror.
I can conquer any Goliath that attempts to come into my life.
I run the race of life as a victor.
I Am victorious like the greats of old who understood courage.
My confidence propels me to new heights.
I AM courageous!
I Am that! That is who I Am!

Thoughts, Revelation, Prayers

Thoughts, Revelation, Prayers

Thoughts, Revelation, Prayers

Thoughts, Revelation, Prayers

Prayer for Peace

Have you ever experienced a moment of true peace? Think about a moment when you were content and accepting of your life. Not necessarily happy about your circumstances but generally, at peace with your life. How did that moment of peace feel?

God wants us to live a life free from strife and worry. He wants us to experience peace that "passes all human understanding." Put your life in God's hand and exchange your worry for His peace!

The Lord will give strength unto his people; the Lord will bless his people with peace.

-Psalm 29:11

I AM PEACE

I Am peace!

I Am free from strife!

I Am in harmony with life.

Today I Am determined to remain calm and centered because everything in the universe is for me.

Even when it appears that I AM in the midst of strife, God gives me his peace.

His peace is sufficient.

I Am whole and I Am complete.

There is nothing broken or missing in my life.

I Am determined to walk in peace with everyone I meet.

Nothing offends me and I worry about nothing.

People enjoy being around me because wherever I go, peace and goodwill appear.

Where there is confusion, I provide clarity.

Where there is chaos, I provide order.

I Am kept in perfect peace because my heart and mind are fixed on God-like things.

My heart rejoices and my mind expands as I welcome this great gift of peace.

I boldly proclaim that I Am in harmony with life!

I Am free from strife!

I AM peace!

I Am that! That is who I Am!

Thoughts, Revelation, Prayers

Thoughts, Revelation, Prayers

Thoughts, Revelation, Prayers

Thoughts, Revelation, Prayers

Prayer of Thanksgiving

Thanksgiving is not a one-time event. Every day you are blessed to walk this earth is a day for thanksgiving. Sometimes the cares of this world can overwhelm you and you feel that there is more against you than there is for you. However, take joy in knowing that your life is a gift from God. When you find yourself complaining about what is going wrong, send up thanks for all that is working well in your life.

"And let them sacrifice the sacrifices of thanksgiving, and declare his works with rejoicing."

-Psalm 107:22

I AM THANKFUL

I Am thankful!

I Am grateful!

I Am appreciative!

Oh God, I give you thanks!

You are good and your loving kindness is eternally present in my life.

Just as the star guided the shepherds to the Christ child, so I Am today guided by the spirit of thankfulness.

I will give thanks today and every day for you have done great things for me.

Thankfulness sustains life.

I breathe! I Am thankful!

Thankfulness perpetuates goodwill, enhances relationships, and fosters friendships.

I love and receive love! I Am thankful!

The life I live is the result of thankfulness.

I Am alive! I Am thankful!

Someone favors me with a gift of kindness and I reciprocate with a smile of gratitude.

I am appreciative for the extending hand that guides me through the shadows I encounter.

Being thankful keeps me centered because I realize without that helping hand to raise me up, challenging situations would be more difficult.

Every moment, of every second, of every minute, of every hour, of every day, I Am thankful!

I Am that! That is who I Am!

Thoughts, Revelation, Prayers

Thoughts, Revelation, Prayers

Thoughts, Revelation, Prayers

Thoughts, Revelation, Prayers

Prayer for Love of self

Love you may have experienced pain and trauma that have caused you to doubt your appearance. Maybe you were abused, or lived through a divorce. Perhaps no one in your family ever complimented or validated you. Today you have the power to declare to the world that you are enough and you are loved! You are a perfect specimen. Embrace your earth suit and live with appreciation for your beautiful body.

> *"And let the beauty of the Lord our God be upon us..."*
>
> -Psalm 90:17

I AM BEAUTIFUL

I Am beautiful! I Am excellent!
I Am magnificent! I Am lovely!
I Am wonderful! I Am delightful!
Yes! This is all me!
When God created me, he broke the mold!
I Am one of a kind.
I look in the mirror and see the reflection of my Father.
I am precisely carved in His image and likeness.
I love God! He does not make mistakes!
I love me!
I see the beauty of the universe in everything around me.
The wind blows as I pass and the trees clap in joyful abandon.
From the crown of my head to the sole of my feet, and everything in between, I Am an extension of God's goodness.
Because God is enough, I Am enough!
I take into myself the glow of the rising sun and feel the warm rays of God's love flow out of my body and energize me.
My beauty goes way beyond what is touched.
There is nothing to compare to my beauty.
I smell the rose and marvel at its fragrance and I smile and whisper "We are beautiful."
The light that shines out of me brings warmth to every dark and damp place.
Today I exercise my ability to change lives by allowing the world to see I Am beautiful!
I Am that! That is who I Am!

Thoughts, Revelation, Prayers

Thoughts, Revelation, Prayers

Thoughts, Revelation, Prayers

Thoughts, Revelation, Prayers

Prayer for Entrepreneurs

God's desire is for His children to live an abundant life. A successful business is part of your abundant life. Throughout the Bible, references are made about God blessing the works of your hands.

As an entrepreneur, you have a special gift in your hands that God wants you to share with the world. Do not be afraid to ask God to send you paying clients and customers. Open your mouth and confess your good success.

*The Lord shall command the blessing
upon thee in thy storehouses, and in
all that thou settest thine hand unto;
and he shall bless thee in the land
which the Lord thy God giveth thee.*

-Deuteronomy 28:8

I AM SUCCESSFUL

I Am successful! I Am extraordinary! I Am prosperous!

Everything my hands touch today is successful.

I Am achieving victory and accomplishing all of the great plans God has for me.

God has given me ideas and concepts to bless all families of the earth and I gladly share those ideas with the world.

I Am overflowing with ideas to take my business to the next level.

My business meets a need and I Am prepared for the demand.

I envision having a triumphant day.

I seek God's wisdom on pricing, marketing, and management for my product/service and He freely gives me what I request.

Those who need my product/service come to me and are willing and able to compensate me for my time and energy.

Just as a farmer plants seeds with an expectation of a harvest, I also sow my talents and gifts knowing I will be financially and spiritually increased.

I allow my mind to travel to places of unlimited heights.

I fill my heart and mind with thoughts of success.

I follow my blueprint of high achievement.

I keep my heart and mind stayed on my anticipated end.

I Am overflowing with wealth, happiness, joy, peace, friendship, and love.

I AM successful!

I Am that! That is who I Am!

Thoughts, Revelation, Prayers

Thoughts, Revelation, Prayers

Thoughts, Revelation, Prayers

Thoughts, Revelation, Prayers

Prayer for Faith

The Bible encourages us to "walk by faith and not by sight." Your life is a series of faith-filled moments. When you went to take a shower today, you expected water to come out of the pipe. Therefore, by faith, you turned the knob. When you sat down on your chair, you assumed it was going to hold your weight. Therefore, you sat down.

Think about all the involuntary actions you took today. They all required faith. Take that faith into every decision you make today. Decide to believe God for the best and be full of faith!

O love the Lord, all ye his saints: for the Lord preserveth the faithful, and plentifully rewardeth the proud doer.

-Psalm 31:23

I AM FAITHFUL

I Am faithful! I Am confident! I Am self-assured!

The faithful shall abound in blessings.

Today I Am abounding in blessings because I Am confident in whom I Am.

I Am confident that God has only good thoughts towards me.

He has plans for my life that exceed my greatest dreams.

I believe because I Am alive, I can do anything I set my mind to do.

I step out to greet this magnificent day full of confidence and hope.

I think thoughts of "I can!"

For I am certain today that I Am able to demonstrate my ability to accomplish any task before me.

I Am faith — strong, immovable, enduring faith.

My faith propels me into unknown realms of peace and joy.

I Am the epitome of faith.

Faith gives me the conviction to pursue all my desires with the firm belief and resolve that I am invincible, I Am unconquerable faith.

Today, I use my faith to move mountains of doubt, insecurity, lack, and fear.

There is a sureness with which I walk and talk because I know who I Am.

I AM faithful!

I Am that! That is who I Am!

Thoughts, Revelation, Prayers

Thoughts, Revelation, Prayers

Thoughts, Revelation, Prayers

Thoughts, Revelation, Prayers

Prayer for Love From Others

Love is a reciprocal process. In order to receive love, you must be willing to give love. The Bible says, "For God so loved the world that he *gave*...." Love is the greatest gift you were ever given. Even to this day, God is still giving love to you.

You have the power to create love for yourself by giving love to others. Some people think God has forgotten about them. Make a decision today to show the love of God to someone who needs it.

Beloved, if God so loved us, we ought also to love one another.

-1 John 4:11

I AM LOVED

I Am loved! I Am appreciated! I Am liked!

As I stand here, face to face with my reflection, I see the love of God.

God loved me so much, He gave me the power to love others and be loved.

I begin this wonderful day by giving myself permission to give and receive love.

Rays of love exude from my being and everyone I come in contact with, feels the warmth of God's love.

I experience love by connecting with my spouse, children, family, friends, and co-workers.

God's love for me supersedes every situation that comes across my path.

Love is the conduit I use to transmit peace and kindness.

My desire is for everyone I meet to experience great joy.

I open my heart and give love away.

I Am love. I express love.

I send love and it returns back to me in abundance.

I have feelings of fulfillment, excitement, and joyous expectation as I proclaim this love.

God's greatest command is to love.

Today and every day, I love.

I AM loved.

I Am that! That is who I Am!

Thoughts, Revelation, Prayers

Thoughts, Revelation, Prayers

Thoughts, Revelation, Prayers

Thoughts, Revelation, Prayers

Prayer for Comfort

Have you ever felt alone but then, as if out of nowhere, a friend calls, or a comforting song comes on? God is always looking out for you. He sent you to this earth with everything you need. Sometimes you cannot see Him intervening in your life, but He is always there. Not only is He there, but He is also covering and comforting you through every situation. Just like a blanket provides warmth when it is cold, God covers and secures you through life's trials.

Yea though I walk through the valley of the shadow of death, I will fear no evil: for thou art with me; thy rod and thy staff they comfort me.

-Psalm 23:4

I AM COMFORTED

I Am comforted.

I Am relieved.

I Am consoled.

Yea though I walk through a valley, I Am increased in greatness and comforted on every side.

God is my comfort.

Today I am thankful for relief from challenges and adversity.

I know I Am never alone.

I Am surrounded by a shield of love.

Just as a mother consoles and quiets her newborn, God sheds His peace and security over me.

I relax in the newness of the day and embrace the serenity that I feel anchored in God.

Today, wellbeing, relaxation, relief, ease, and luxury are my constant companions.

God is my refuge and a very present help in times of trouble so I fear nothing.

I AM comforted.

I Am that! That is who I Am!

Thoughts, Revelation, Prayers

Thoughts, Revelation, Prayers

Thoughts, Revelation, Prayers

Thoughts, Revelation, Prayers

Prayer for Guidance

When you travel or go on vacation, you may need a tour guide. The guide knows everything about your vacation destination. You believe what they say and follow their lead. That is how God wants you to live your life—following His lead. Sometimes things won't make sense, but He wants you to trust Him. Understand, it is in God's best interest for you to reach your expected end. He won't steer you wrong!

*And the Lord shall guide thee
continually, and satisfy thy soul in
drought, and make fat thy bones and
thou shalt be like a watered garden,
and like a spring of water, whose
waters fail not.*

-Isaiah 58:11

I AM DIVINELY GUIDED

I Am divinely guided.

I Am directed.

My steps have been ordered.

Where ever God leads me, I will follow.

I place my foot in His footprints and walk confidently knowing I am being lead and guided through every moment of my day.

I place my confidence in His ability to protect me, my family, and anything that concerns me.

Whatever happens today, with God, I have the ability to walk through valleys of disturbance, unrest, or misunderstanding.

He lights my path with His brilliance.

I trust in God with all my heart and lean not on my own understandings.

In all my ways I acknowledge Him and He directs me.

God's wisdom is my wisdom and I Am always in the right place at the right time.

My obedience makes way for my success.

I AM divinely guided.

I Am that! That is who I Am!

Thoughts, Revelation, Prayers

Thoughts, Revelation, Prayers

Thoughts, Revelation, Prayers

Thoughts, Revelation, Prayers

Prayer for Confidence

Confidence starts from within. If you do not believe in yourself, how can you expect others to believe in you? God created you with special gifts and talents. There is no one else in the universe exactly like you. You were sent to earth with a special assignment that only you can fulfill. There is an entire world waiting for you to live up to your fullest potential! There are problems in the world and you have the solution.

*For the Lord shall be thy confidence,
and shall keep thy foot from being taken.*

-Proverbs 3:26

I AM CONFIDENT

I Am confident!

I Am self-assured!

Cool, self-reliant, poised, and certain are the words that describe me.

Today I am all those things and more.

I Am confident!

I walk secure in my image, talents, and gifts.

I know who I Am!

The confidence in which I Am makes me poised and prepared for new opportunities.

I rise like a phoenix above all situations.

Today, everything and everyone is working on my behalf.

Nothing happens to me.

It happens for me.

I Am as confident as the waves.

I know when to rise and when to lay low.

I Am confident like the oak that knows how to bend with the wind but never break.

I run into my destiny with strides of purpose because confidence attends my way.

I AM confident!

I Am that! That is who I Am!

Thoughts, Revelation, Prayers

Thoughts, Revelation, Prayers

Thoughts, Revelation, Prayers

Thoughts, Revelation, Prayers

Prayer for Spouses

God's intention is for you to enjoy every aspect of your abundant life. Your relationships are an integral part of that abundant life. An important relationship is the union between husband and wife. Being married to a person you love and having that love reciprocated, is a blessing.

However, relationships like marriage require commitment and special attention. Having a successful marriage means being the best spouse you can. Make a decision to be everything your husband/wife needs.

And the Lord said, it is not good that the man should be alone; I will make him a help meet for him.

-Genesis 2:18

I AM A WONDERFUL SPOUSE

I Am a wonderful spouse!

I Am a great spouse!

God gave me the gift of a wife/husband and I appreciate my gift.

Every day I experience joy from my relationship.

No weapon formed against my union shall prosper.

Today, I take the time to nurture this blessing called marriage.

I pray that my wife/husband fulfills her/his purpose in life.

I put forth my best effort and energy to create an environment where my wife/husband feels secure and loved.

I experience great pleasure from seeing my spouse's physical, spiritual, and emotional needs met.

As I give to my spouse, they return my love

and affection without limitation.

I sow seeds of love and reap a harvest of joy,

laughter, forgiveness, and passion.

My relationship is filled with all things good and lovely.

I Am blessed.

I Am loved.

I AM a wonderful spouse.

I Am that! That is who I Am!

Thoughts, Revelation, Prayers

Thoughts, Revelation, Prayers

Thoughts, Revelation, Prayers

Thoughts, Revelation, Prayers

Prayer for Parents

Being a parent is an honor. You have the opportunity to mold and shape the mind of a future inventor like Thomas Edison or a future world changer like Martin Luther King, Jr. The possibilities are endless. God has entrusted you with His prized possession and He equipped you with every necessity to care for that life.

Parenting may not be always perfect, but it is rewarding. Enjoy being a co-creator with God! Embrace your role as a parent.

As arrows are in the hand of a mighty man; so are the children of the youth.

-Psalm 127:4

I AM A LOVING PARENT

I Am a loving parent!
I Am a caring parent!
I Am a successful parent!
I have been given the gift of parenthood and I Am honored.
I look at my hands this morning and realize I have the ability to change the world through my children.
My children are the future and I take the time to nurture their minds and spirit.
I have everything I need to be a good parent to my children.
God has equipped me with love, patience, forgiveness, kindness, understanding, and sensitivity.
Whatever my children need to live an abundant life, I freely give to the best of my ability.
Where I lack wisdom, I ask God for knowledge and it is given.
I realize I have the power to speak positive words into my offspring.
I speak that they are strong, anointed, intelligent, and beautiful.
I have been given seeds to plant and water.
Today, I nurture these seeds to greatness.
My children are a blessing to me and everyone they meet.
I ask for angels to protect my children and keep them safe.
I AM a successful parent!
I Am that! That is who I Am!

Thoughts, Revelation, Prayers

Thoughts, Revelation, Prayers

Thoughts, Revelation, Prayers

Thoughts, Revelation, Prayers

Prayer for Seeking a Spouse

A man who finds a wife finds something very precious. In addition, a woman who is found by her husband receives great love. There is nothing wrong with desiring a life companion.

He/She who finds a spouse, finds a good thing. In seeking a spouse, remember to become the type of mate you are looking for. Are you looking for someone who is honest? If so, you must master being honest. Are you are looking for someone who is generous? Then practice being generous. There is a mate looking for the good things you have to offer.

Whoso findeth a wife findeth a good thing, and obtaineth favour of the Lord.

-*Proverbs 18:22*

I AM A SEEKER FINDING A MATE

Today, I look around and expectantly make space.
I make room for the person assigned to compliment me on this journey called life.
I Am willing to adjust.
I remove all obstacles from my path.
I Am a diligent seeker.
Like the lame man at the pool,
I Am willing to take up my dream and soar.
I Am a seeker.
I seek love, romance, friendship, passion,
truth, peace, and companionship.
I Am a finder because I know the diligent seeker always finds. So today I ask for companionship.
I seek companionship and I find companionship.
He/She who seeks diligently finds a good thing!
I Am a good thing and I attract a good mate to me.
I AM a seeker finding a mate!
I Am that! That is who I Am!

Thoughts, Revelation, Prayers

Thoughts, Revelation, Prayers

Thoughts, Revelation, Prayers

Thoughts, Revelation, Prayers

Creating Your Own "I AM" Statements

Join the "I Am" movement by creating your own "I Am" statements.

1. Start by selecting an area(s) or aspect of your life where you want to excel. For example, maybe you are looking to be a better parent or increase in your finances.

2. Find applicable scripture references that address the area(s) by using a Bible concordance. Look up the word(s) that best describe what you want to be, have, or experience. Common examples would be: parent, peace, wealth, marriage, joy, health, healing etc. Use the scriptures as a guide when writing your statement.

3. Use a thesaurus to find synonyms for the words you selected in step 2. This broadens your language for your "I AM" statement and provides multiple ways for you to state your "I AM."

4. Write out the scriptures you selected in step 2 and add "I AM." Example: Psalm 112:3 says, "Wealth and riches will be in this house, and his righteousness endures forever." Your "I AM" statement may read like this—"I AM wealthy! Wealth and riches are in my house and my righteousness endures forever. I AM wealthy!"

5. Use 4-5 scriptures to create your "I AM" statement.

6. Do not be afraid to call yourself what you want to be.

7. Start your "I AM" statement strong and become who you say you are!

Write Your Own "I AM" Statements

I AM…

I AM…

ABOUT THE AUTHORS

Dr. Lucille P. Farrell-Scott ministers the Word of God with dynamic power. She is committed to the work of God and her ardent desire is to see the lives of men and women changed for the better.

Dr. Farrell-Scott ministers to families and the restoration power of God is seen over and over again as homes are restored and hurting families are healed. Experiencing a devastating divorce has given Dr. Farrell the heart "to minister to families and nurture them back to wholeness."

Dr. Farrell-Scott is an educator, motivational speaker, transformational coach, author, entrepreneur, and renowned lecturer throughout the world. She has studied psycho-spiritual dynamics for over 40 years and teaches on the principles of meta-physics.

Other books by Dr. Farrell-Scott:
Surviving Single Parenthood
Awaken the Leader in You

Dr. Sunne-Ryse S. Smith is a consultant, trainer, inspirational speaker, and author, and professional mentor. She is the founder and lead consultant for Inspiration Matters, LLC; a consulting firm that specializes in supporting newly formed non-profits, school systems, and entrepreneurs in developing powerful programming for the communities they serve. As a former public-school executive, ordained minister, and school psychologist she combines her unique professional and personal experiences with her passion for inspiration to help people live a full, purposeful life.

She has been featured in *Essence* magazine with her mother for their powerful work together. She has also appeared on news programs and various podcasts as an expert on emotional well-being.

Dr. Sunne-Ryse holds degrees from Lincoln University (PA), and Fairleigh Dickinson University. She is most proud of the education she received from being a mother to her 2 beautiful children, and a wife to her husband of 17 years.

Other books by Dr. Smith:
Spiritually Woke

www.ingramcontent.com/pod-product-compliance
Lightning Source LLC
Chambersburg PA
CBHW060400080526
44583CB00012B/410